Chinese Blisters

My Trek of the Great Wall of China

Jane Waugh

First published in Great Britain in 2008
By Jane Waugh

ISBN-978-0-9556895-0-5

In memory of those I have loved and lost to cancer.
Sadly too many to mention.

Contents

The Way Forward

How many times have we heard the saying *"there is always someone worse off than you?"* I had recently met someone whom I admired and wanted to seize an opportunity before it passed me by. It also gave me the chance to give something back to others less fortunate than myself. The person in question shall remain anonymous for two reasons, one being that I have never met her again since our time in hospital together and two, I don't recall her name.

We first met in outpatients, she, an old hand at the pre-op assessment and me an ignorant, terrified rookie. When she spoke to me her face seemed slightly lopsided and the lines on her face advanced for her years. I later discovered she was not much older than me but had had many operations on her face and neck and many of her wrinkles were in fact fading scars. Like me she had been diagnosed with tongue cancer, unlike me she had undergone massive facial and jaw operations to remove the persistent tumours and was returning yet again for reconstructive surgery.

We chatted like old friends the first time we met and she put my mind at rest that we had a top surgeon working on us. Relieved to know she would be there when I arrived nervously at the hospital the following morning and to find her ensconced in the bed opposite.

By the time we left two days later, both slurring our words and dribbling, I felt very humbled that I had spent this traumatic time with someone so brave. That was one of only two operations I have had to remove small cancerous lumps from under my tongue and touch wood will remain that way. She on the other hand will have undergone many more painful days of recovery and if she ever gets to read this journal and recognises herself I wish her all the luck in the world.

My dentist had investigated a white scaly patch on the underside of my tongue and I had been referred to a maxillo-facial surgeon. Since then I had undergone several biopsies and the two operations over the last few years. Unfortunately the last set of results had come back with cancer cells and so I had the operation to remove them. If you have ever bitten your tongue by accident you can imagine how painful my recovery was. I had many stitches and could not speak very clearly for a while.

It was whilst recovering from this operation in May 2002 that I read an article in a magazine about a trek on the Great Wall of China. The article was written by a woman who was about to take part in the 2002 trek and the brief read:

"If you would like to spend six days walking through the hills surrounding Beijing and alongside the Great Wall, the next trek is scheduled to take place from 8th-18th April 2003. Call for an information pack"

The trip was organised by Breast Cancer Care, a charity close to my heart as I had friends and relations who had been affected by this cruel disease. For the rest of that day I kept returning to the article and wondering if I should give it go. I eventually decided to send for the details and see what was involved.

The dreaded C word has touched many people's lives. I had lost my father, uncle, grandmother and a very close friend of 21 to the disease in its differing forms and felt lucky that I had a chance to recover and was now healthy and able to get on with my life. This opportunity had been given to me to do something not only to help others but also to give me a goal to work towards and achieve something for myself.

The following day I mentioned it to Sandra, a very close friend and found to my amazement that walking the Wall was also one of her ambitions. Within the week I had received the pack from Breast Cancer Care and the two of us had spoken to Celia, a friend who had suffered with breast cancer herself. She expressed a great interest in the challenge and also sent for the relevant information from Breast Cancer Care.

When my pack arrived we looked through it carefully and over a glass of wine on Sandra's terrace, we decided to go for it. We debated whether our other halves would cope without us for ten days and I rang my Mum, to see if she would lend me the £250 deposit to secure my place. Another recovered patient to the disease herself, she was more than grateful to help out and gave me the money as her sponsorship donation.

The trek involved joining a group of approximately 70 other people and walking on various parts of the wall for 6 days. Each day would throw up a different challenge. The trekkers would be from all walks of life and attempting the trek for varying reasons.

We posted our applications that afternoon and by Friday 17th May we had been accepted and were on our way. Our Trek was booked for April 8th – 18th 2003, only eleven months away.

An Earlier Life

When I left school in 1976 I went to Bulmershe College in Reading and trained in PE and Sports management. I was then employed as a squash club manager for several years where I met my husband Patrick in 1980. After being made redundant I joined British Airways at Gatwick until I changed careers in 1986. Pat and I travelled a lot for the first 8 years together, visiting Australia, USA, Indonesia, Israel, Europe, Gambia and islands in the Caribbean.

I was employed at British Airways when Pat and I married in December 1985 and as I was an airline employee we went on honeymoon to St Lucia at a fraction of the cost. Pat also visited his brothers in USA on the strength of this and was very disappointed when I handed in my notice to join the West Sussex Ambulance Service in 1986. I worked as a technician for the service for many years and was one of the first female employees in West Sussex to start paramedic training in November 1991. The training was very intense and tiring and when I discovered I was pregnant, was advised by the doctor to go onto light duties and continue my training after the baby arrived. Motherhood won me over and I never returned to complete my final two weeks of hospital training.

My first child Josh was born in May 1992 and I returned briefly to the service until my daughter Ali was born in June 1994. Due to there being no provision for female employees having child care needs I found it impossible to return and resigned.

Since having the kids I have worked part-time as an auxiliary nurse both on the wards and in the outpatient department. At present I work with the under fives, supervising activities and helping in the crèche at the local sports centre. My present ambition is to train in some form of sports medicine and to have my own business.

Although studying at college in Reading for three years I have always lived in Mid Sussex, firstly with my parents in Sedgwick and later with Pat in Horsham, Cowfold and now Warninglid. We live with our two kids Josh 9 and Ali 7, Mollie the bad beagle, the cats, Diva and one eyed Ziggy, and Louise the guinea pig, in a Victorian cottage we are quickly out growing. Close friends, Sandra and Steve, also live in the village in a converted pub with their two boys, Mike and Christopher and dog Ella. The two families met through the children and have since spent many holidays and weekends together.

Sandra worked in a financial establishment in the City of London where she met Celia, someone who was to become a very close and treasured friend. They kept in touch over the years and although Celia and her husband Gerry never had children, she was devoted to Sandra's two boys. I had met her on a couple of occasions but did not know her well. Sandra often talked fondly of her and I was soon to get to meet her a lot more.

Working up a Sweat

In April 2002 Sandra completed the London marathon in 4 hours 20 mins and is super fit, so I have a lot of catching up to do fitness wise before the China Trek. Better get a move on.

I started my fitness regime straight away with a three-mile walk with the family and the dog. On Monday the boys from Warninglid School were partaking in a sports day at Ardingly College, a local public school, so we dropped them off and took the dogs for a walk around the nearby reservoir. This took about 1 hour 40 minutes and covered about 6 miles. Guess what? I had a blister at the end of it. These trainers will have to go.

During the week I took the dog out every day and then on Friday we did another 6 miler through Freechase Estate. This is a large house and grounds in the village of Warninglid with footpaths all around it. It was to become a very good training walk as it is hilly, rough in places, and quite exhausting. It is one of the prettiest walks near to us and over the next few months I was to become very familiar with the terrain and the wildlife. At the moment the woods are carpeted with bluebells and everything is looking incredibly green and spring like.

The following week I covered over 20 miles with Mollie, my faithful training partner of the next few months. We are both definitely getting fitter and she loves the hikes through the mud.

In order to take part in the trek we had to pledge to raise £2500 each. This amount seemed daunting at the beginning but as fundraising was something we have been involved in for quite a number of years we had lots of ideas as to how we were going to raise our £5000.

Both Sandra and I had been on the school PTA where we had held numerous fayres, discos, balls and children's events so the prospect was not too intimidating. We decided to try and hold one event a month and involve different groups of friends and family in each event. A list was drawn up and we started by seizing the moment and taking advantage of 'World Cup Fever'

Fund Raiser No.1 - World Cup Sweepstake

As our first fund raiser we organised a World Cup Sweepstake. This meant selling a ticket for every team partaking in the football tournament. We charged £5 for each team and sold all of them in the school playground and to family within the first week. The winner was obviously the person who had picked the team that triumphed in the World Cup and they inherited £50. Everyone enjoyed watching his or her team play during the rounds and the eventual winner was really chuffed.

One of our major fundraising ideas was to write to everybody we knew. This involved drafting out a letter on Breast Cancer Care headed paper and writing a begging letter to all our family, friends and acquaintances telling them what we were about to do and why. We then waited and hoped they were all feeling generous.

Shortly after I wrote this letter I heard the shattering news from my sister that her husband Nick had just been diagnosed with a rare form of cancer. He had discovered a small lump in his neck whilst shaving one morning and it had grown enormous almost overnight. He had had it checked out and they had confirmed that it was indeed cancerous. Sadly, yet another member of our family affected by this persistent disease.

Both Nick and I are under 45 and neither of us has ever smoked. I am grateful that my treatment is hopefully over, whereas Nick has to undergo a massive operation in a couple of week's time. We both make monthly visits to the oncology clinic in Brighton, which despite the nature of the place always seems very relaxed and everybody seems very positive.

Jubilee Scotch

10 months to go

Celia and her springer Amber came down to stay over the Jubilee weekend so the three of us did our first training walk together. We completed the Freechase loop in about 1hr 30 mins, the three dogs got on famously and we really felt that we were on the way. During the walk we discussed backpacks, bottled water, trousers versus shorts and sleeping arrangements.

Celia had a double mastectomy a couple of years ago so she is one of our main reasons for wanting to help this worthwhile charity Breast Cancer Care. My Mum is also a survivor of breast cancer and has passed her seven-year check up with flying colours. My Grandmother on Mum's side was not so fortunate and died of the disease a couple of months before my wedding in December 1985. My grandfather gave me her wedding ring to have as my own and I treasure it with my life.

Fund Raiser No.2 - Jubilee Fayre

During the Jubilee celebrations in the village of Warninglid where both Sandra and I live we had a stall selling badges, draw tickets, balloons and various other Breast Cancer Care items. Sandra's husband Steve has a duty free business and he very kindly donated a fabulous Jubilee Bottle of Scotch Whisky which we sold tickets for. Celia was on great form and looking fantastic. She is full of life and her old bubbly self it's fantastic to see her fighting fit. Throughout the afternoon we sold over 120 tickets and then during the evening the draw was made. The winner of the whisky very generously gave the bottle back to us to auction and we made a further £115 profit, £235 on one bottle of Scotch.

This event gave us a lot of encouragement and we realised we had a great deal of support. Everyone was very interested to hear of our adventure and offer advice.

During the first month of our fundraising campaign I received cheques to the value of £430 in the post and will be eternally grateful to those people for giving us the support we needed so early on. I have had some extremely generous amounts of money from some of my friends and acquaintances and it just proves how many people this cruel disease has affected.

We have organised several other ongoing events to help us raise money and not a day goes by when I do not think how lucky I am to be planning this trip of a lifetime. Pat and the children, Josh and Ali have been brilliant. The kids have donated some of their pocket money and are very encouraging towards my training. They are however getting a bit fed up with falling over trekking magazines and boot surveys. Ali insists she will miss me loads when we go in April but Josh thinks it will be cool not to have Mum around for a few days nagging him to tidy up his belongings.

9 months before

It is now July and while I am typing this, the rain is pouring down outside. Sandra is sunning herself in Spain with the family and I am trying to think of some other ideas to raise money. I think a wine tasting evening would go down well, any excuse for a drink and a get together with friends. I will go and do some research on the idea while it is fresh in my mind. It's too wet to take the dog and the kids out walking, I'll wait till Pat gets home and the weather has cleared up a bit.

I telephoned a local guy in the wine business and he is willing to do an evening for us with quizzes and tasting and lots of wines to buy at the end. Sounds just what we are looking for and he has promised not to charge for his services as it is for such a good cause.

Since Sandra has been away I have done some 4 and 7 mile walks, dodging the showers where possible. The weather has been atrocious, it never seems to stop raining and it is getting very depressing. Where is summer?

I have received several more cheques in the post, one from an old friend and employer whom I hadn't seen for years.

One good thing to come out of writing to lots of old friends and family we have lost touch with is getting back in contact with them and taking up where we left off. Pat and I had dinner out with some friends on Saturday whom we hadn't seen for ages. It was fantastic to catch up on all their news, they were however upset to hear of Nick's problems, and wish him a speedy recovery.

I have just banked up our first lot of funds with Ellie in the Breast Cancer Care office. This amounted to £1020 between Sandra and me and with our £250 deposits we are well on the way to our first £1000 each.

Fund Raiser No.3 - Head Shaving

On the last day of term Josh very bravely agreed to have his head shaved and raised a staggering £140 in sponsors. He was a bit nervous before the event but thought it was really wicked. Practically the whole school stayed to watch the event and everyone was giving us money, some of the kids were even pledging their pocket money. He looked a bit anxious as the clippers burst into action but took it all in his stride. He went from looking very young to several years older in a matter of minutes.

Many thanks to Sandra's sister for coming down to school and performing this task on stage for us. I hope it doesn't take too long to grow back; at least we have the school holidays ahead of us.

It's Pouring in!

During the school holidays the kids and I went through the telephone directory and made a very long list of companies, family attractions, local gardens, and restaurants and sent them all a letter telling them what we were hoping to do. We asked them if they could send us vouchers or tokens to help in our fundraising.

We had a fantastic response and have arranged a silent auction for later in the month and a large raffle to be drawn in December, the first prize being a Virgin Balloon Flight. Nick, who has been unable to use the balloon flight himself due to his treatment, very kindly, donated it to us. Pat has done a very professional looking brochure for the Auction and we have sent out dozens listing all the items on offer and are hoping for a great turn out on the night.

Many companies responded positively to our letter, too many to mention. A huge thank you also to everybody who helped us with donations, special thanks to friends and family who donated their time or items for the auction.

6 months before we leave

Now October and we are well on the way to completing our fundraising. It's now been several weeks since I have had the time to sit down and continue this document, but guess what? Yes, it's pouring with rain and Pat is at work and the kids are watching a video. The summer months have been and gone with hardly any sunshine and we are now enduring the long dark evenings and gloomy days. I often wonder why we live in this country; I'm definitely a summer person and get quite depressed over the winter.

Nick has had his operation and completed six gruelling weeks of radiotherapy. He now awaits the consultants' verdict next week to see what will happen next. While resting at home during and after his treatment he has dug the hole for the family swimming pool. You can see what a determined chap he is.

Fund Raising No.4 - Silent Auction

Well the Auction day has arrived and although we have given out loads of brochures and told lots of people about the auction we are both very apprehensive about the event. Not knowing how many people will turn up on the night and how much money they will want to spend.

We arrived at the local village hall at 13.00hrs armed with all our donated goodies and started setting up tables. Once we had laid out everything with the appropriate cards, put up posters about the China walk, opened a bottle of wine (for Dutch courage of course) and blown up dozens of balloons for the kids, we sat back and waited for the crowds. Some of the auction items included:

- a case of Chardonnay
- extra large chocolate bars
- a mountain bike,
- Spanish lessons
- dinners for two
- cameras
- teddy bears
- books
- food hampers
- bag of daffodils
- fitness training session
- videos
- jewellery
- perfumes
- season tickets to local gardens
- offers of baby sitting and ironing

- various entry tickets to shows and attractions
- and many more

An hour later we were still waiting, but from then on we had a steady flow of locals, school friends and acquaintances and never looked back. The evening went really quickly and lots of people from the village whom we had not met before came down to show their support. Everybody was very generous and every single item, over 60 in all, had a bid on it at the end of the event. In total we had raised over £1400 on the donated items and taken a further £400 on raffle tickets and pledges.

We were overwhelmed by every ones generosity and hope all the vouchers and tokens lived up to expectations.

Once all the monies from Friday have been collected, we shall be sending Ellie a massive cheque, which will take us way over our £5000 target. Not bad in only 5 months, now we can concentrate on the training programme we have set ourselves and look forward to meeting up with the rest of the group in February.

Walk this Way

Our next fundraiser is a coffee morning to be held at Sandra's in November, now we can relax and enjoy our friends and neighbours company with no pressure to raise extra money. The raffle ticket sales are still going well, with the draw taking place on 7th December.

A few weeks ago I decided (at long last) on which trekking boots to buy and they are now well broken in. A very good choice, lovely and comfortable from day one and oh! So stylish with their little paw print laces. The day-sack however is proving more of a problem. Some are good looking but not the right size, others are the perfect fit but don't come in the right colour, and some are perfect but too pricey.

Celia came down today; she is doing really well at the moment. We took the three dogs for a walk over Freechase and they had great fun together. Mollie managed to get the muddiest despite the fact that she won't go in the water. She will however find the wettest route from A to B and loves every minute of her time out. Amber is a bit of a mummies girl and she and Mollie have a love, hate relationship. Mollie chases her around and she cowers round Celia's legs. If she dares to go ahead of Mollie at any stage of the walk, Mollie will bark and overtake her – she does like to be the leader of the pack. Now Ella is getting a bit slower she hates it when a new pup comes along and tries to steal her thunder.

Having not done any long walks for a while because we have been a bit inundated with auction organising it was lovely to get some exercise and some fresh air. It was a gorgeous day although very cold. We walked for hours and the dogs were almost good buddies when we got home.

I'm off to Shropshire, youth hostelling, with my old college crowd at the weekend. No doubt they will all be waiting to hear about our forthcoming adventure and we will have a long walk organised by Pete our intrepid orienteerer. I shall probably come home exhausted, over fed and having drunk too much wine, but hey, you only live once.

Despite a long tedious drive to Shropshire we had a great weekend and it was lovely to get back with the old college crowd and their families. Several of us did the same PE course at Bulmershe and have become friends for life. We now meet every year during the autumn half term and take over a whole youth hostel. Normally there are about 21 of us but each year we have a few dropouts. Sometimes the Dad's can't get time off work and most years one or two of the kids have commitments which stop them coming. We have been doing this since the year Ali was born so this will be our eighth time and we have stayed in about six different hostels all over the country. We have revisited a couple of the better ones, which are well located for everyone, as we all come from different parts of the country.

Well, I survived the weekend, despite the storms and a power cut which started early Sunday morning and was still going on when we left on Monday lunchtime. We managed a long, hilly, strenuous walk on Saturday, organised by Pete. The weather was beautiful, sun shining, not too cold and no rain. We walked for about 4 hours with several snack stops to keep the children going. The youngest was Harry who is 5 and he was only carried once throughout the day when we took a wrong turning and had to go back up a very steep hill.

Sunday night our numbers had depleted a bit due to work and school commitments on Monday, but those of us that remained enjoyed a candle lit dinner followed by an early night with our candles to show us the way to our dormitories. The kids' thought it was brilliant fun and told ghost stories to one another well after all the adults had fallen asleep exhausted.
All in all a great weekend with good company; we all promised to take candles with us next year and repeat the candle lit dinner

as it was so atmospheric. Next year we will in fact all be going over to France for the gathering as one of the couples have just become the proud owners of a farm near Limoges and have invited us all there for the half term break.

No Gain without Pain!

5 months and training hard.

I have ordered an aero walker, which I hope will be delivered tomorrow. I then have no excuse not to do any exercise when the weather is really bad and can improve my stepping technique for the Great Wall trek in April.

Well the stepper eventually arrived a week late and I am now training every other day on the gravity walker, stepper and with free weights. When I first started on the aerobic stepper I found it very tiring work and managed about one minute at a time.

Now it is the beginning of November and I am doing ten-minute sessions. The gravity walker is much easier and just gets monotonous after a while – I do about 25 minutes on it with the radio on full blast and imagine I am trekking the Great Wall! The weather has been so dreadful that getting the enthusiasm to go out and walk for any distance is not easy, but the dog has to go out every day so at least I do a short walk.

Have suffered a bit of a set back with my tongue cancer in that I found another white patch that needed a biopsy. More stitches and horribly painful for most of the week, but now healing well. My speech seems to have been affected since my operation in April and each time they chop a bit more out it seems more slurred. Most of my family and friends say they don't notice it, but I get quite self-conscious of it.

Had to wait a couple of weeks for results and then visit the oncology clinic in Brighton. My appointment came through and I discovered that Nick's appointment time was ten minutes after mine at the same clinic. We were both given the good news that everything was OK for now and we have to return in a month's time for check ups. Patrick was with me and my sister Sarah with Nick so we went out for a celebratory lunch. Nick's voice is still quite husky after his treatment and his neck is still stiff, but he has complete movement in his shoulder and arm, which is brilliant news. He is very positive about the prognosis and is living life to the full. He tells a wonderful story about a shark attack if strangers or kids inquire about his scar.

Fund Raiser No. 5 - Coffee Morning

Since last sitting down and writing this diary Sandra and I have had our coffee morning and raised another £120 for Breast Cancer Care. It was a relaxed morning with lots of friends and neighbours dropping in. No hard sell from us but still a successful fundraiser. We are now over our £5000 target and working towards the next £1000. We still have the raffle draw, which will take place tonight, we have sold over 320 tickets and all the prizes were donated so have made another £320 pure profit.

The fund raising, although hard work and quite time consuming has been lots of fun. We have talked to loads of people about the trip and so many of them have been affected by breast cancer, either themselves or close relations. It is very humbling to be part of something that will assist so many people less fortunate then us.

Breast Cancer Care is an amazing organisation who provides a service to those having to face up to the diagnosis of breast cancer. This service is for the patients and the families and friends of patients to talk over their fears and answer their questions. They offer emotional support and practical help and the sponsorship money we raise will go directly to ensuring improved access to this support. Over 4000 women and 300 men in the UK are diagnosed with this type of cancer every year.

Down but Not Out

Devastating news from Celia today, she has just found out that she has secondary cancers in her breastbone and lung. She is now having chemotherapy for the bone cancer and will shortly be undergoing more treatment for nodules on her lung. Sandra and I are both praying that she will successfully fight this and be able to come with us to China for our challenge. She is a fighter and I'm sure she will get herself fit. She is a very positive person and I know like myself, having had something important to focus on over the last few months has helped keep her going. She has a very supportive sister Julie and her Dad and husband Gerry will be there for her too.

Celia has also surpassed her fundraising target and still has money flooding in. Between the three of us we have now accumulated over £10,000.

Yet another wet weekend is upon us, we have all the lights on and it is only lunchtime. Will go out later with Mollie and get wet and cold, but hey, it's all for a good cause.

Have received some great e-mails from fellow trekkers and think that maybe I should be upping my training. Is everyone aiming to be superhuman for this walk and am I going to be left behind at the first hurdle. Is my little gym in the conservatory enough to get me fit or should I be joining the local fitness club and training everyday?

One of the e-mails mentioned they would like details on how we put the silent auction together, it really was a good profit-making evening, with every item donated. I will send details to them.

Before I had my children I was an ambulance technician with West Sussex Ambulance Service and have kept in contact with a few of my colleagues. One of them, Jerry, has now set up his own business as Southern Medical Services and he provides paramedic and first response cover at sporting events and shows around the country. I worked for him as an emergency medic a few times last year at The Oval Cricket Ground. It has been suggested that I approach Jerry as a sponsor for the trek and get him to supply some form of medical kit for the three of us. We might be able to get some publicity for the company if we do an article for the local paper.

Later in the month Sandra and her family are off on yet another holiday – this time to spend Christmas with her husband Steve's family in Singapore and then onto Australia for New Year with Sandra's brother. They will be away for a month and we have agreed to look after their German Shepherd, Ella for the duration. Her bed takes up most of the dining room so Christmas morning should be interesting. She and Mollie, our beagle get along famously and love their walks together.

Fund Raiser No. 6 - Grand Raffle

Well the raffle has been drawn and Sandra's neighbour Sally won the balloon ride – she seemed very pleased. The other prizes were spread around the county and have now all been dispatched. Sandra phoned Sally at about 10.55pm to tell her the good news and managed to wake her and her husband up. We were sat round the dinner table downing another bottle of wine and didn't realise the time.

After the very wet weather we have suddenly been plunged into winter with serious threats of sleet and snow. Monday dawned clear and bright so I decided to go on a long walk with Mollie. We set off on our usual 6-mile trek around Bolney and Spronketts Lane and then added on Freechase. The sun was still shining when we got back into the village although it was bitterly cold. As it was such a glorious day I decided to return back home the long way round and added another 3 miles to the walk. When we eventually returned, after about 3 hours, we had covered 10.5 miles.

Wednesday was also a dry day, very cold with a bitter wind but Sandra and I took the dogs out and managed to walk and chat over 5.5 miles in just over an hour. I have been onto the local Ramblers web-site and found some great walks to do in January, February and March. We will have to sign up with them first and then look forward to some different routes. Some of their rambles are on the South Downs Way so they should be quite challenging.

Hairy Mary!

4 months till D-day

Celia has just finished her first three weeks of chemotherapy and now gets a week off. She is also visiting the plastic surgeon today to check out the pain she is getting, hope this is nothing to serious, she has enough to cope with at the moment. Even if she is not up to walking in China, Sandra and I remain determined that she will come with us, and see Beijing and The Great Wall. When Celia had her chemotherapy before she lost all her hair and was extremely unwell. She is obviously not looking forward to this happening again; it must be so much harder the second time around, as you know what to expect.

Sandra is now in full holiday mode; I am very envious of her having 4 weeks in the sun, while we shiver over here. I wonder what Christmas in Singapore will be like?
They have a fabulous apartment on the Darling River in Sydney over the New Year and then go up to Hamilton Island on the Great Barrier Reef.

Well into December now and the Wescott's have left us for sunnier times. We are suffering more wet miserable weather. Have just returned from walking the dogs over the fields, it takes almost as long to wash and dry them down afterwards. Ella loves to go in the ponds over the fields so she is lovely and muddy when we get back. She has settled very well and is no trouble. Our two cats, Diva and Ziggy are not too keen on our large hairy guest and are behaving very badly.

I have sent some more cheques up to Ellie at Breast Cancer Care headquarters; have now banked well over £6000 between the two of us. I received lots of information on the 'Trek' in the post and have decided to extend our trip to include some shopping time in Beijing after the walk. Sandra's sister in law, who lives in Singapore, is hoping to come and meet us at the end of the trip so it will be exiting to spend some time with her.

I am looking forward to getting the full itinerary in January from the tour company. I have read several reports from people who have done the walk before and are eager to compare routes and accounts with those. I must remember to fix an appointment with the doctor to see if he recommends any jabs before we go. Sandra also needs to sort out her medication for asthma so she has supplies on her if needed.

Christmas is now only days away; the kids are very excited. We collected some holly over the fields yesterday, which always makes the house look festive. I wish the weather would buck up, I love it when it's cold and bright. Not much chance of snow this Christmas

I have had several text messages from Sandra, telling us what a great time they are having. Also a couple of phone calls to check on Ella. The weather in Singapore was wet and very warm but I think it's better now they have moved down to Sydney for the New Year. Just received a text wishing us a happy new year, they are off to bed and we still have our evening at Ruth and Kevin's to look forward to. Pat is on an 8-4 shift today and then a long 12-hour day tomorrow. He will know doubt be tired and not up to partying the night away.

New Year's Eve afternoon and Ella has left us for a farm in Balcombe. Helen, a running friend of Sandra's picked her up yesterday. They have a large house with a scullery where they can clean the dogs down and dry them off. Ella has been no trouble at all but because it has been so very wet, rubbing her down and keeping the house remotely clean has been very difficult. Mollie is still sulking that Ella has gone elsewhere and even went off eating for about five minutes. I would happily have her back during the summer months.

Dress Code

I have had some information in the latest Breast Cancer Care pack which made good reading.

"A visit to China is the trip of a lifetime. Third after Russia and Canada in size, it is second to none in population (more than a thousand million) and extraordinary variety, more like a continent than a country. The north borders Siberia, while the south is well into the tropics. The fertile flood plains of China's huge rivers are intensively farmed; it's deserts as wild and empty as anywhere on earth.

The Great Wall is roughly 80kms from the centre of Beijing. Northwest is the most visited stretch of the wall, at Badaling Pass. The Wall stretches over 6300kms from east to west. The trip telescopes history, from the modern capital, through the outskirts to where donkey carts and cargo carrying bicycles share the road, past farms where nothing seems to have changed for centuries, to harsh mountain ranges where nearly a million workers walled in an empire."

We were also sent a copy of the suggested packing list:-

- T-shirts – 1 per day
- Thick natural walking socks – pair per day
- Walking boots with good ankle supports – they should be worn in!
- Walking shorts and lightweight trekking trousers
- 2 sweaters
- Lightweight jacket
- 2 sweatshirts
- Casual attire and change of footwear for the evenings
- Hat
- Gloves
- Daypack

- Toiletries
- Toilet roll
- Towel
- Swimming costume
- Tissues and wet wipes
- Compeed plasters
- Small first aid kit
- Torch
- Lip salve and sun screen
- Insect repellent
- Energy bars, dried fruit, Kendall mint cake or dextrose tablets
- Polythene bags for dirty washing
- Small knife
- Notebook, pens, diary
- Small padlock
- Spare passport size photographs
- A copy of your insurance certificate
- Money belt

Optional

- Camera gear
- Binoculars
- Reading material
- Walkman
- Games
- Sandals
- Sleeping bag liner
- Walking pole

Pack as lightly as possible!

Not your usual holiday packing list but then again as I keep reminding everyone and try to convince myself this is not a holiday but a hard, arduous trek which is going to challenge the best of us. Difficult to remember when I have never visited China before and still see it as such a great adventure and a chance to broaden my horizons and add another country to my list of places visited in the world.

I haven't done any walking since the kids broke up and now Pat is on 12-hour days it will be next week before I can do any long spells out with Mollie. I have been doing some training in my mini gym with the weights, stepper and gravity walker. Josh is doing a charity 5000m (200-length) swim in March so we are going to go and do some swim training together when the term starts. He is swimming for Cancer Research and hopes to raise over £100 in sponsors.

I have e-mailed Ellie about extending our stay after the walk, hope we will get places. I shall be very disappointed if it has filled up over the last couple of weeks. Must phone Celia and see how she is getting on with her chemotherapy, she and Gerry may be coming down to stay at Sandra's while they are away. Hope she is keeping positive and keeping up the fight.

I have now got my daysack sorted and bought! It holds 20 litres and is very stylish and has all the necessary.

I have received lots of bits and pieces for the trek in my Christmas stocking. I am now the proud owner of a Maglight, Swiss army knife, portable washing line, key ring, sleeping bag liner, socks, spare laces, mirror and Compeed plasters! What more could a girl need. I am getting very excited about the trip, can't wait to meet up with everyone in February and compare notes.

Chinese Sayings

Over the last few months I have read a couple of novels on travelling in China. Adrift in China by Simon Mayers was very good, about some guys that travel across China on their motorbikes and the people they meet on the way. He says on the back of his book and I quote - "In such an extraordinary country it is easy to get lost" He should know! The other, Red Dust by Ma Jian was a bit heavier going but still very interesting. Have been looking at some of the Chinese phrases we have been given and getting nowhere. I seem to be having problems with the pronunciation, especially with my occasional lisp. Must try and learn some of the lingo before we go, even if it's just some basic stuff.

See what you make of some of these:-

- Hello – Ni hao
- Goodbye – Zaijian
- Thank you – Xiexie
- How much is it? – Duoshao qian?
- What's the time? – Ji dian?
- Toilet – cesuo
- Telephone – Dianhua

See what I mean!

I have just done a good workout, now walking and working out on alternate days and really enjoying it. Mollie and I did a great 10-mile walk on Saturday, it was exceptionally cold but I managed to get a sweat on going up Freechase Hill! New set of weights arrived on Monday and Ali and I had a really good session with them – it was too cold to go into the 'gym' so we took over the dining room. A bit sore on Tuesday. I will do a new 10/11-mile walk tomorrow round Bolney, Wineham, Twineham and Warninglid. Don't know if Mollie will be impressed as it's all on roads, but it is still so wet underfoot. Have spoken to Celia, she seems in good spirits and is coping particularly well with her treatment.

We had a bit of a hiccup with our money situation. I received a receipt from Fiona at Breast Cancer Care and our funds had gone down since our last lot of cheques were received! Soon sorted out and we have now raised £6397 between the two of us. Have spoken to Emma about extending our stay in Beijing and she has reserved us places. I am now getting somewhat excited about this trek, it is only 13 weeks away. I seem to spend all my spare time leafing through brochures and web sites seeing what else I need to get before we go. I have my 45th Birthday in February so hopefully will have my final list together before people ask me what I would like.

Lovely day yesterday so I dragged the family out to walk Wolstonbury Hill, near Hurstpierpoint. This is one of the steepest hills around here and Ali and I managed it without too much huffing and puffing. Josh was very glad to get to the top and was then content to go down hill the rest of the way.

Have since done another 10-mile walk, again it was very cold when I set off so it's difficult to know what to wear. Started off with hat, gloves and fleece, but after an hour was down to a sweatshirt! Went to Crawley on Thursday and bought a Helly Henson wick T-shirt and a micro-fleece top so should now be better equipped. Sandra back from Australia tomorrow so will be organising some walks, maybe with the local ramblers.

3 months remaining

Another 10 miler on Monday and dropped in at Sandra's on the way home. They all looked horribly fit and well and made me feel very pale. Had a fantastic time and were finding it extremely cold in England – they should have been here last week.

As I hadn't had any news from Celia I feared the worst about her condition and I'm so sorry to say that Sandra confirmed my fears after she spoke to her on Tuesday.

Down And Out but Still Fighting

The specialists have told her there is no way she will be fit enough to come and walk the Great Wall with us, or to come and experience China without trekking. She has to face a lot more treatment and possibly surgery and they are not being very optimistic about her prognosis. Celia is obviously very disappointed and concerned about her condition but she must do all she can to keep herself as stable as possible.

Her sister Julie, whom I have never met, has agreed to take her place on the walk and between the three of us we are now more determined than ever to succeed in this challenge. Julie has been a tower of strength to Celia over the last few months and they are a very close family unit.

Sent my registration form off to the tour company for our Beijing extension on Friday and had a look at the Exhibition Hotel web site. It looks really pleasant, should be fun to have an extra couple of days for shopping and relaxing before we come home.

Now swimming twice a week after work on a Tuesday and Friday, a bit of a nightmare as the pool is quite busy but sometimes I get a free swim if the receptionist is feeling generous. The slow swim lane is a bit tedious for me as I keep catching up with people infront of me but the swimmers in the fast lanes pound up and down so quickly I wouldn't have a chance! Maybe when I've been a few more times I'll brave the faster lanes. I'm swimming for 30mins and doing an average of 32 lengths.

Dug out my aerobics tape last night so will also try and do that a couple of times a week with my weights. Enjoying all my exercise but am pretty tired by the end of the day.

Ali is pestering me to climb Wolstonbury Hill again so I had better go and keep her amused. She swim trains several times a week and is a member of a junior triathlon club so is very fit! We are off to some friends tonight to catch up on all the news and hear about Steve and Sandra's holiday. Had a lovely walk but got lost up on the Down's and ended up climbing over barbed wire after cutting through a sheep's field. Eventually got home, to find the boys hadn't noticed we'd been gone!

The weather has been incredibly wet again and we have also had more snow. Sandra and I were ready for our first 14 mile walk last week but the day was very black and heavy snow was falling so we ended up at Sandra's drinking coffee and sorting out our lists of things to do for China. We did feel a bit guilty but at least we kept warm and cosy and her son Mike was off school sick so we couldn't have gone far anyway.

Have been doing weights and aerobics twice/three times a week, but have had to hang fire on the swims. I have had a ghastly cold for the last ten days, which still shows no signs of going. Must get back into full training on Monday, only nine weeks to go now.

I have now made a list of things to ask at the meeting on Saturday, really looking forward to meeting everyone and also getting to know Julie whom I still have not met up with. Had a phone call from a fellow trekky, Lesley Taylor in Burgess Hill last week. When I returned her call she was in the middle of her step routine, made me feel guilty for having had a day off.

Had some gruesome photos taken at the booth at the supermarket this morning, they went straight in the bin! Why do those passport photo pictures make you look like you should be in jail or in your coffin? Sorted out the visa forms and got the postal orders from the post office. I must look out my passport and list of questions for next week.

Trek to London

2 months left to go

Travelled up to London on Saturday for the Trek meeting, arrived quite early and met up with a couple of fellow trekkers, one of whom, Sandy, had come from North Wales and the other from Yorkshire. Eventually made our way up to the fourth floor and waited for the rest to arrive. Met Julie and immediately felt like I'd known her forever, so like Celia and very easy to get along with.

Had an interesting meeting with lots of information, photos, videos and chat, all of, which was extremely useful. All the questions I had on my list were covered by the tour rep, she has done the Trek three times before, and was very informative and told us exactly what to expect. Came away feeling very excited and wanting to go now! All the trekkers are very enthusiastic about the trip and looking forward to meeting again at the airport at the start of our adventure. Sent love and hugs to Celia with Julie and promised to email each other soon with any news.

Had my typhoid and hepatitis A jabs done on Monday, both completely painless have booked up tetanus and polio for a month's time.

Glorious day today so put on my hiking boots and off Mollie and I went. Hiked the usual 10 miles and then added on Slaugham, which after I had picked up the kids from school and we had walked home gave me a total mileage of 13.5. I took it very easy today as I was still suffering from this wretched cold which will not go away. Ali seems to be coming down with it now as she fell asleep on her bed when we got in. Will try and do the same walk with Sandra and Ella on Thursday. Feeling a bit tired now but luckily we have no clubs to go to tonight, so once the kids are fed and watered I can relax and put my feet up.

Well, two weeks down the line and I have done zilch. Have been suffering with a horrid flu like bug, which has really wiped me out. Had my usual swim after work on Tuesday, but was struggling after 5 lengths. Managed to complete the 40 lengths but was exhausted afterwards. Took Ali to trampoline club and fell asleep at the side of the gym. The rest of the week was a wash out and my Birthday came and went without celebration. Pat worked a 12- hour day and both the kids were at school until 4.30pm. Saw no-body all day and felt thoroughly miserable. Cancelled lunch out with Mum and the girls and have put a hold on going to Zizzi's for supper on Saturday.

Helped out at the school Jumble sale on Saturday morning and did the Tesco shop in the afternoon but this all wiped me out for another few days. Eventually started feeling normal again on Friday and returned to work. Took Mollie for a 5 mile walk on Saturday and then took the kids out to eat in the evening as my Birthday treat.

Kids on half term next week so will have to do some gym workouts and bike rides and swims with them, really must try and get back into exercise mode, only six weeks to go!

Josh and I have completed a nine-mile walk around Slaugham and Freechase. Didn't think he would make it all the way round but he kept up well and was fine until he tripped and fell in a very muddy wet puddle at about 7 miles. Josh well deserved his roast supper and a couple of hours in front of the telly. Sandra's Birthday tomorrow, so will be going round for a glass of something and a sandwich at lunchtime. Oh to be 39 again!

Had a lovely time at Sandra's, all the girls wanted updating on the trip. I had earlier completed the Slaugham walk with both the kids. Josh was not really in the mood and lagged behind – not really a training walk, although Ali and I could have gone much further, only did 5 miles in total.

Still waiting for my walking pole to arrive, has been over two weeks now. Look forward to using it and getting used to it before we go. Only 5 weeks to go now. I have now bought my journal, which I will start at the airport and fill in every evening while we are away. Always kept a diary when Pat and I travelled a lot before we had the kids and it is great to look back at them and remember all the things we did and the different places we visited.

The walking pole has arrived and it's very posh. Can't wait to put it to the test, but the weather is not too good and the kids are not very keen on going out. Saturday will be the first trial. Pat and the kids are going to his Mum's for the majority of the day so I shall do a long walk with Mollie. Went down to Slaugham and then into Freechase. The pole was very useful, as it was so muddy. Once I got the hang of using it, it stopped me falling in the mud on several occasions. Had a strenuous walk although we got caught in the rain and came home soaked. My fleece top managed to keep me dry, even though my jeans were soaked through. Mollie had a wonderful warm sudsy bath when we got in and then ran around like a fluffy puppy for the rest of the evening.

Met Sandra and Julie on Sunday and did a 7 mile walk around the lanes, after yesterday we decided it was just too muddy to go over the fields and woods. Weather was idyllic and we all got pleasantly warm, spring is in the air at last. Had an engaging natter about the trek and decided on what we were going to be taking with us. Julie is insisting on taking her hair dryer. All excited about the trip getting closer, but really heartbroken that Celia will not be accompanying us. Making us all the more determined to complete the challenge for her. Julie has a personal trainer coaching her through her paces although she doesn't have a lot of time to walk as she works full time. Arranged a couple more weekends when she can come down and walk with us, and maybe Celia will be able to come down too.

Walked around Slaugham on Monday and back across the fields to school, then back up to Connor's to pick up Josh after he had ridden there after his cycling proficiency course. An enjoyable walk and I'm now doing it in a very much quicker time.

More Bad News

1 month nearer

On Thursday I did a new walk which I drove in the car first. It seemed quite a long, hard walk but it turned out to be perfect and it was a fantastic sunny day and a really pleasant temperature. As it was all on the roads it was hard on the feet, but very enjoyable. At least the boots didn't take too long to clean.

Ali has sprained her ankle and Pat is working a long weekend so I won't be walking over the next few days.

Two more jabs on Monday morning and then a good long walk for the rest of the day. Only 4 weeks to go! Julie and Celia are coming down at the weekend and we are hoping to meet up with Lesley and some of the others to do a couple of long treks.

Spring has sprung and the weather is fantastic. Lovely, warm sunny days, although it's still frosty at night. Have done a few 7 and 8 milers, Celia and Julie came down on Sunday and we did a steady Freechase hike. Celia kept up pretty well but was coughing a lot and a bit wheezy. Lovely to see her despite the fact that she has had still more bad news she was in good spirits.

Since having a further MRI scan last week they have discovered another tumour, this time in Celia's brain. She is very anxious about everything and it is really hard to know what to say or do for her. I guess we just have to be there when she needs us but it is very difficult for Julie and Sandra.

Did some last minute shopping with Ali on Monday and have got the rucksack down from the loft to do a dummy pack! Must sort out the money side of things and get some Chinese Yuan and travellers cheques ordered from the travel agents.
Seem to be working quite a lot at the moment, so time is very

precious. Start my new job at the Meadows Surgery with the emergency doctors on Monday evening. This involves working nights and weekends driving the on call doctors to sick patients. It fits in well with Pat's shifts and brings in a bit of extra cash.

Received my passport back from the Chinese Embassy on Friday, now has a smart new Visa in it! This pneumonia that is in the Far East is a bit worrying – we will have to get hold of some surgical masks to wear on the plane if the situation gets any worse. What with that and war about to break out in Iraq it will be a miracle if we ever get to China. We now have less than three weeks to go and I'm counting the days.

2 weeks to go

Sandra and I took the dogs and went for an exhilarating walk up on the South Downs. We started at Jack and Jill windmills in Clayton and followed the footpaths for several miles. Neither of us knew where we were going but we went up towards Ditchling Beacon and then back along to the windmills. We had some lunch in the car park and decided to do another walk down towards Keymer and then back up the hilly bit. Sandra had run this route twice as a fun run so had a rough idea where we were going! It was a beautiful sunny day and the temperature was perfect for walking. The route up the side of the hill was very steep and when we stopped for a breather and a drink poor old Ella collapsed in a heap. We were wondering how we were going to get her down or up the hill when she had a second wind and off we went. Hard work but well worth the views and we both felt better for it afterwards.

Celia is due to undergo invasive gamma ray surgery on her brain tumour next Tuesday so had further scans done yesterday to see if there were any more problem areas. She and Gerry have taken off to Norfolk for the rest of the week to chill out and relax, if that is possible in the circumstances.
Celia now home after her surgery; they found two more tumours

but the operation seems to have been a success. She must be so brave to be coping with all of this so well, I don't know that I could be.

I have really eased off the walking this week, due to having so much else going on. Picked up my Chinese money and travellers cheques this morning and got some last minute shopping out of the way.

Must remember to get the kids some Easter eggs before I go and hide them well. Haven't yet decided on plans to get to the airport, Tuesday is a busy evening for the kid's activities so maybe it would be best if Pat were here to ferry them around. Sandra is arranging a drinks get together for the weekend before we go, just so we can see the gang and say farewell. Need to read through all the Breast Cancer Care info on the trip and make sure I have everything sorted.

Spent a couple of hours at work today reading through all the Breast Cancer Care literature we have accumulated. Makes very interesting reading and has really got me in the mood. Only ten days to go. Ali is at Lucy's for a sleep over and Pat has just gone to bed after nights so Josh and I are off round Freechase. Glorious sunny day and it was so peaceful in the woods, saw four deer and lots of other wildlife.

Been sorting out my first aid kit, Sandra and Julie reckon they have their own private paramedic travelling with them so I had better come up with the goods if need be! Josh was a bit tired walking today so it took us a long time to get round! I will do it again tomorrow.

1 week before we leave

Weather is fantastic at the moment, so we are all making the most of it. The forecast in Beijing is not so good, quite cool and some rain, may have to rethink my packing.

SARS has hit and I received a panic phone call from a friend in Hong Kong. She and the children are coming home to escape the deadly virus and she is telling me we should not be travelling to China.

I contacted the tour company and Ellie at Breast Cancer care, they both assured me there is NO PROBLEM IN BEIJING and the trek is going ahead. Watching the news headlines and reading all the reports in the papers. Feel that any time now the world health organisation will stop people travelling to China unless it is vital. Australia, Canada, France and later USA are all advising people not to go to China on holiday but the British as usual seem to think it is OK. We are being told to be aware of the symptoms and take precautions, but there is no need to cancel.

Have been to the hospital and got surgical masks for the three of us! Still very worried about the situation, it has definitely put a damper on the week. We should be really excited but we are concerned that if we go we could bring the disease back with us and endanger others. Everyone I have spoken to seems to think it would be better not to go, but we have received nothing from Breast Cancer Care to say that they are even considering postponing the trek. I guess we will go and hope for the best.

4 days and counting

Friend from Hong Kong came by with the kids, and brought a supply of masks for us to take with us. Still saying we are mad to be going and that the situation is much worse than the media over here are letting on. She says Hong Kong is a ghost city with all public places having been shut and everyone who dares to go out covers their faces and avoids other people.

3 days to go

Meeting up with the gang at Sandra's for a drink tonight, no doubt they will all have their opinions about the SARS situation. Must start to get myself organised and get my gear ready to pack. Simon, Julie's other half is taking us to Heathrow on Tuesday evening so that Pat can sort out the kids and their various clubs.

Orient Express

The day we have been waiting for.

Well the day has finally arrived and for the first time ever I am nervous about travelling. Maybe it's because I'm leaving Pat and the kids behind or maybe the world situation with SARS and Iraq has something to do with it?

Packed up and everything fits in. I will be wearing my walking boots as I don't want them going astray in a lost bag, anything else I can beg, steal or borrow but my boots could not be replaced at this short notice. Pick the kids up from school and gets lots of good wishes from everyone. Simon picking us up at Sandra's so go straight there from school. Goodbyes are horrid and not looking forward to saying them to the kids.

Very good run up to Heathrow, traffic amazingly well behaved for the M25. We arrived in just under the hour, so nice and early. We all felt a bit more relaxed now and strolled into the terminal to check in our bags, thanking Simon for the lift and promising to keep him up to speed with our progress. The terminal is quite quiet and we soon found our check in desk.

Away We Go!

Day 1 Tuesday 8th April 2003 - Breast Cancer Care Information:
Air China scheduled economy class flight CA938 departs for Beijing at 20.25hrs. Total flying time approx. 9 hours. In flight entertainment is mostly in Chinese, so please bring along a good book or magazine. Dinner and breakfast served during the flight.

There are no queues, so we hand over our bags and are now ready to go to the departure lounge. Send a quick postcard to the kids so they remember me in a couple of day's time when they receive it. We met up with Lesley and her friends in the Costa Coffee bar and see lots of other trekkers milling around the lounge. Meet up with Jacqui, Julie's friend from the golf club. It is her first time away from her husband in 30 something years so she is a bit apprehensive. Also meet Paula who is another lady on her own and she and Jacqui seem to hit it of.

Sandra drags us all to the bar so she can get her daily gin and tonic fix. Flight is called on time and we have now met up with the Breast Cancer Care girls, Fiona and Jo, Richard the doctor, and Lou the tour representative. All seem very friendly and I'm beginning to relax a bit and look forward to our adventure.

China Air

Day 2 Wednesday 9th April 2003 - Breast Cancer Care information:
Arrive in Beijing 13.10hours. Pass through security check, visa and passport control and collect luggage. Wait with the group at the luggage carousel. Once everyone has their luggage, exit the Arrivals Hall as a group. Meet the representative from our Land Agents CITS, who will have a sign saying "BCC – China Trek". You will be transferred by coach for a drive of approximately 2 hours to the Jinshanling Lodge, our hotel in the countryside. This is close to the starting point of our first day's trekking. Welcome briefing for the following day.

The flight is long, cramped and uneventful, the majority chatting, reading and sleeping most of the way. We eventually arrive and meet up in the baggage reclaim area. Lesley is looking anxious, as everyone's bags seem to have come of the conveyor belt except hers.

We eventually find Lesley's bag has gone to Hong Kong by mistake and they will try and get it to her as soon as possible! Luckily she is travelling with three friends who are roughly the same size, so she manages to borrow clothes for the few days she is without it and by some miracle one women out of 70 has a spare pair of boots and they happen to be in Lesley's size!

Lots of the Chinese people are wearing surgical masks but we feel brave enough not to bother at this stage. There was nothing said on the flight about the situation and there were no health checks when we got off the plane.

Our luggage is left outside the airport and we are assured that it will meet up with us at the first nights accommodation. We reluctantly leave it with some Chinese people we have never laid eyes on before and board two coaches which will take us on the first stage to our Lodge at Jinshanling. Everybody is pretty tired by now as few got any sleep on the plane and the journey through the Beijing suburbs is quite monotonous although some of it is interesting. Our first glimpse of China and its people, I can't believe how tiny they all are!

The journey continued through the outskirts of Beijing which went on for miles and miles all looking amazingly similar to the previous miles and miles. The houses all looked the same, the landscape was all very familiar and the people all looked alike. The buildings looked unlived in and almost derelict, with no glass in the windows and curtains as doors. Every house was identical to the one next door and there was no individualism at all.

The rooves were corrugated iron and then as we got further into the farming regions most of them were covered in hay bundles. This was the way each family dried out enough grass for their livestock. All the buildings were the same drab grey colour and the landscape was dull scrubland. On many of the roadsides we saw a Chinese person with half a dozen sheep grazing right on the verge. How they escaped being hit by the many tourists buses passing them I'll never know. The animals were beautifully cared for and seemed very healthy, often more so than the people tending them.

One part of the journey took us over a stretch of about 2 miles of unmade up road which was extremely treacherous and kept us all wondering whether we would ever make it to our destination. The official road was being repaired so the diversion was set up around it through tracks and off road paths. A 4 x 4 would have been a better mode of transport, but it all added to the adventure of being in China and doing things the Chinese way.

Eventually arrive at Jinshanling lodge and are greeted by the 'Hello People'. They are the locals who want to act as guides and bag carriers for us over the next few days and become firm friends with some of the trekkers and a nuisance to some of the others.

Found our rooms and happy to discover that the three of us have been put in together. First impressions were not good and Julie was soon on the phone texting Simon to get her a flight home! Sandra was looking for the laundry bags so she could get her travel clothes washed and ironed and I was inspecting the room for creepy crawlies.

We had two rooms connected, one of which was very, very damp and the other just damp. We took the mattresses off the bed in the very damp room and put it on the floor in the less damp room. With the heating on full blast we reckoned we might dry it out before bedtime. We sorted out some clean clothes and Julie headed for the shower. She soon returned saying she didn't feel that grubby afterall and she'd wait until the morning when it was lighter. There was actually no light in the bathroom worth mentioning and the floor was permanently covered in a layer of slimy water. We all decided we would be cleaner if we stayed as we were.

After a couple of hours phoning home and lounging about we made our way over to the restaurant for supper. We then discovered we had one of the best rooms in the lodge and some people had no heating at all. Our first Chinese meal was well worth waiting for and consisted of several courses of delicious vegetables, noodles, cooked meats and rice. We were all feeling extremely well fed and settled down to a few beers and a good chat with all the people at our table.

Lesley's friends turned out to be three sisters, one of whom had recovered from breast cancer and had persuaded the others to come with her on the trek. They were lovely ladies and we were to spend a lot of time with them over the next week or so. We also chatted with the doctor, we had a gamble on how old he was and the winner bought the beers with her takings. Several of us were old enough to be his Mum.

We eventually rolled into bed a little worse for wear, only to wake in the night and have to turn the heating off. We found out next morning at breakfast that Jacqui and Paula had had to share a bed to keep warm as their room was like an icebox. We did feel a bit guilty.

The First Steps

Day 3 Thursday 10th April 2003 - Breast Cancer Care information:
Breakfast in the hotel dining room. Participants to meet in hotel lobby area. Please be dressed in trekking gear – we recommend long trousers, as you will be walking through some areas of undergrowth. Take your small daypack for personal belongings, packed lunch and water supply. Today's trek will be from Gubeikou Great Wall to Jinshanling. After breakfast transfer by coach (20 minutes) to the Great Wall at Gubeikou. We start by walking from the entrance up to the Wall. Once on the Wall we trek for about 2½ hours until reaching a point where we come off the Wall and walk to a local village. From here we will hike back to Jinshanling Lodge.
Total trekking time 4-5 hours. Briefing on the following days trek, dinner and overnight at Jinshanling Lodge

After a very good breakfast we went back to our rooms to prepare ourselves for our first days trekking. As it was very cold we decided on trousers and fleeces and the old faithful walking boots were about to get their first taste of real wall trekking. We met outside and all picked up boxed lunches and four bottles of water. That put a bit more weight in the old rucksack and I was glad I had been carrying it around fully laden on my walks back home. We clambered aboard the coaches and they took us several miles back down the valley to Gubeikou.

Here we had our warm up exercises, led by Carol our Chinese guide. We all felt very self conscious as we were doing them on the side of the road and all the lorries passing were hooting at us jumping up and down. At last we set of and walked up to the wall. The wall at this point was virtually non existent and was just a rubble path with no sides to it. The path was covered in undergrowth and shrubs and the walking was quite hard work. Some of the 'Hello People' had now found themselves a buddy and many of them were helping our fellow trekkers by carrying their rucksacks and guiding them over the rough terrain.

At this point we also met our two video girls who trekked most of the way with us and always appeared at the top of the towers waving and shouting "hello" to us as we clambered up the steep bits of the wall. They were both delightful and were so full of energy – they kept infront of us all the way and took some great footage of the trek for us to keep as a memento.

Unfortunately the weather was rather misty and the cloud was very low, so the views we had been looking forward to seeing were not visible. I managed to fall over the side of the wall at one stage and had a quick visit to Mongolia. I was putting Sandra's water bottle back in her rucksack when she turned quickly and knocked me over into the ditch on the Mongolian side of the wall. Luckily Julie wasn't prepared with the camera so we have no visual proof of this unofficial visit.

We trekked for about two and a half hours and then came off the wall and descended into a valley. This was our first lunch stop. Some lovely scenery to be seen this morning but a backdrop of blue sky would have made it better. Lots of stops for photos and for the stragglers to catch up as there were some very steep sections in and out of the towers and a few people were struggling.

Our lunch boxes were interesting, consisting of salad rolls, bananas and peanuts, but to be honest we were all ravenous and ate most of it. Julie and Sandra experienced their first pee in the woods, the first of many I might add.

The descent into the village was very steep and hard work on the knees. I actually found coming downhill much harder than going up hill. The afternoons trek was through a remote village where we saw life in rural China at its best. The whole family was involved in the ploughing of one field, which was amazing to watch. The men would steer the horses that were pulling the plough and the women would follow behind sowing the seeds. After them came more male members of the family covering the seed with the soil and then some more people to tread down the soil. In all about 14 people were doing a job that in more mechanised countries one man and his tractor complete.

As we entered the village the weather closed in on us and it started to rain quite hard. Guess what the 'Hello People' had for sale in their ever-expanding carrier bags? Correct, plastic rain coats and hats! They sold a few to the trekkers who had been caught out and seemed very pleased with themselves.

The goods they were constantly trying to sell us were very cheap, they had postcards and books of the wall and lots of other souvenirs, and the pennies we gave them probably fed their families for days.

As we went through the village I couldn't help but notice the pride with which each little house had been built. Although only made of stone with thatched roofs they were exquisitely kept and the area outside was immaculate. Bundles of sticks were tied together and propped up against the houses. These were used to light fires under their stone beds to keep them warm at night.

Any animals they had were in immaculate condition and all had shelters to stand under, to keep out of the rain or sun. In one field I had to chuckle when I saw an elderly women on her hands and knees reaping spring onions while her husband stood by leaning on his fork watching her. She looked exhausted and very wet but he made no effort to help her.

After another very steep climb up we made our final descent into Jinshanling village and back to the lodge for that dreaded shower. We all wore shoes while showering and none of us was in there longer than we needed to be, it was the dark brown lump of something in the corner that was most disconcerting and having no light didn't help. Chilled for an hour and then made our way to the restaurant where we were greeted by the 'Hello People' ('HP') with all sorts of different merchandise. They were selling 'pure silk' kimonos, dresses, hats, sweatshirts, fans etc and making a fortune out of the tourist women who hadn't been shopping for a day!

Supper was excellent – not much chance of losing any weight on this trip if they go on feeding us like this. More beers and chat, hit the sack about 10pm and all woke about 3am for an hour, our body clocks are still adjusting.

HP Sauce

Day 4 Friday 11th April 2003 – Breast Cancer Care information

Breakfast in the hotel dining room. Participants to meet in hotel lobby. Please be dressed in trekking gear with your luggage ready to load onto the coach for transfer to Simatai Lodge. Today's trek will take place in full sunshine, with no shade on the Wall whatsoever. We set off from Jinshanling Lodge and walk up to the Great Wall at Jinshanling. Many parts of the wall have uneven steps and some loose rubble but generally it is easy going underfoot – just tough on the legs and lungs! Towards the end of the walk we descend the Wall into the Simatai valley. You will have a boxed lunch on the Wall. Once we have arrived in Simatai we will meet our coach and transfer to the Simatai Lodge where you will be staying overnight. Total trekking time 6 hours. Briefing for following days trek, dinner and overnight at Simatai Lodge.

Pack up this morning and leave our 'lovely rooms,' luggage to be left outside the lodge and taken on to our accommodation for tonight. Setting off from the lodge after our warm up, we were split into two groups. Those who wanted to go at a slightly quicker pace than yesterday and those who were happy with the speed. The three of us opted for the first group as we had found the day before quite tedious. Again a lot of people paid the 'HP' to carry their bags and assist them on the difficult climbs.

The walk up to the wall was long and very steep and took about 40mins. The steps were all intact although uneven. When we reached the top there were a few tourists but we soon left them all behind as we continued on our way to Simatai.

Trekking today was very hard, very rugged under foot, no sides to the wall and extremely steep up and down. Sandra was a bit spooked by the lack of sides, as she is scared of heights if there is nothing to hang onto. Julie and I coaxed her over the hairy bits and she coped very well. Several of the women struggled today but they all made it to the end of the day.

Fantastic scenery and the weather was quite a bit brighter. Awesome feeling looking back where we had come from and a great sense of achievement when you looked back miles over the mountains and realised that you had walked it. We ate lunch on the wall today, just before the border. Cool and windy so sheltered by the sides of the wall.

The section of wall at Simatai was built during the Ming dynasty and has a total of 135 towers. This part of the wall is incredibly steep and some slopes have inclines of 70%. The distance between Jinshanling and Simatai is about 10km but can take 4 or more hours to trek as it is so steep and uneven. This section takes in 30 towers. The towers were built not only as watchtowers but also as places of storage, and as accommodation for the resting soldiers. Some are built on two stories and are elaborately decorated within the brickwork. The views from some of the tower windows are breathtaking and scan vast areas of the surrounding countryside.

Lunch was again interesting with cheese, salad and jam in the rolls! Some long stops for people to catch-up. Chilled down very quickly and had to wear fleeces all day to keep warm. We had a bit of trouble at the Jinshanling/Simatai boarder, as the security police wouldn't let the 'HP'cross, as they didn't live there. Many of the trekkers insisted that they continue with them, as they couldn't manage without them.

Eventually let through and a lot more very steep climbing before we descended down a metal staircase onto a wooden and metal bridge to cross Mandarin Duck Lake. This particular bit was a bit hairy for the girls with vertigo but they all got across, some to the cheers of the rest of us.

A long walk down into Simatai valley and our third night's

accommodation. We checked into our room, which overlooked a lovely courtyard and had views of the mountains above us. Bathroom was clean and we drew straws as to who would freshen up first.

Phoned Celia and had a good chat, seems like she is here with us. Sandra keeps saying how like her Julie is in her mannerisms and speech. I don't know either of them well enough but it is great to have Julie here doing this trek for her sister. Liz, one of our smaller and less able trekkers arrived at the lodge about an hour and a half after everyone else, but was in good spirits.

Wander up to a Chinese restaurant behind the rooms for supper tonight and for some authentic musical entertainment. We enjoyed a fabulous meal, good beers and great company. Sat with Sarah, Alisa and Jo and got to know them a bit better. We discovered that Jo had suffered from breast cancer and that she had also lost her sister to the disease. She is now a picture of health and let's pray she stays that way.

Four musicians came to entertain us after supper but to be honest it was not my cup of tea, it sounded a bit like the kids practising the violin! Back to our rooms for a good night's sleep, Jacqui and Paula also had their first good night since arriving in China and were well rested the next morning.

The Dragons Spine

Day 5 Saturday 12ᵗʰ April 2003 – Breast Cancer Care information
This morning we will transfer back to the Simatai area and trek to the East Section of the Great Wall. We walk for approximately 1½ hours. We then move off the Great Wall and trek to Gangfang Village, from where it is approximately 3 hours trekking back to Simatai where we will meet our coach and transfer back to the Wuzoulou Lodge (about 1½ hours). Total trekking time 6-7 hours. Briefing, dinner and overnight at Wuzoulou Lodge.

We woke to a fabulously sunny day and the most awesome view. Looking up the mountains to the wall running along the top is one of the most amazing sights I have ever seen and one I will never forget. The towers could be clearly defined against a vibrant blue background and the wall snaked around us like a writhing dragon's spine. The turrets on the towers could be seen from a distance and the crumbling sides to the walls looked dramatic.

The Great Wall of China was originally built to keep out marauding nomads and building started as long ago as 221-207 BC. The wall never performed its original function but was used mainly as a means of transporting goods and people across the mountains.

To construct the wall hundreds of thousands of men were used and legend has it that workers that died on site were used as materials within the wall. Much of the wall is now in ruins but some parts have been rebuilt due to the demands of the tourist industry.

Nowadays, The Great Wall doesn't actually exist anymore – instead there are segments of wall remaining, some of which have been restored and some of which are in a state of disrepair.

The wall is not continuous and there are parts of it, which cannot be passed due to the growth of vegetation. Other areas are so badly decayed that they are no longer visible. These parts are only visited by the serious trekker. On the other hand some parts of the wall are beautifully restored and visited by thousands of tourists every day.

After breakfast we packed up our kit and left our clean room for who knows what! The day started with a hike back up to the wall. Where we had come off it last night was where we were joining it today and we all knew this meant STEPS and lots of them! Once we made it up about 200 steps the trek began and what a trek it turned out to be today.

The wall was very crumbly, had no sides to it and was incredibly steep. We were all getting used to this and becoming a bit blasé. We had a pee stop at one of the towers and then started another ascent when a force nine gale hit us and nearly sent us over the wall. We were climbing up the slopes in ones and twos when we noticed Kath, our tour guide, above us yelling at us to keep to the left-hand side of the steps. When we approached the bottom of a run of about 150 steps the wind tore through us at a rate of knots and we had to climb up the side on our hands and knees. Luckily none of us had drunk much water yet so we had a good few litres in our backpacks to weigh us down. I swear some of the smaller, lighter women would have been blown off the wall if not for the weight in our packs and the fact that most of us crawled up this section of the wall on our bellies.

I felt exhilarated when I got to the top, but some of them were really terrified and had felt their lives were in danger. Sandra had been ahead of Julie and I and had been at the top for a while when we reach her. She was still green and shaking, and very scared of what lay ahead. We took a well-earned rest at this spot and took some photos of the views from the towers and of some of the others coming up the steps.

As we came through the next tower the wind seemed to drop and the sun came out again.

After a while we had to climb steeply off the wall into scrubland as the wall disintegrated into nothing and was not passable. Peter, one of our four men out of 74 on the trek, helped every woman over the side of the wall and deserves a medal for his patience. We then descended for about an hour and all met at the bottom, congregating on some poor farmer's immaculately ploughed field. I guess he was compensated by the fact that we picnicked on his land and bought water and snacks from the villagers.

Sandra managed to befriend two little Chinese boys and got a lovely picture of them eating a chocolate bar she gave them. We had a riotous lunch with lots of stress relieving. We then set off UP a steep incline for about an hour before climbing back down into Gangfang village.

Here we saw the local women and children doing their washing in the river, rubbing it clean by pounding it with a stone on a large rock and then washing it in the not very clean water! Again we spent some time talking with the locals, taking photos and relaxing and enjoying the atmosphere of this very charming remote village.

We also saw the local school, which was tidily kept, and had a list of all the children's names inscribed on the wall outside. Further into the village we were met by inquisitive villagers who stood by immaculately dressed and watched us trek through their village to our next destination. Most of the houses were nothing more than shacks, but they were all neat and tidy and most had good luck banners displayed on either side of the front door. It made them very colourful, as they were mostly bright red and yellow in colour.

From the village we trekked along the river bank for about three miles until we came back to the wall which led us back to Simatai lodge and the buses which took us to Wuzoulou Lodge for the night. It was fantastic looking back up to the wall above us and seeing the spot where we had all struggled against the fierce wind a few hours before. Some of the group bought medals with The Great Wall of China on them and with their names etched on the back

Today we had walked for about 7 hours and were all tired but thrilled that we had completed such a challenging day. We had our official group photograph taken outside the restaurant. This took some organising as people kept wandering off. I presume everyone is in the picture I have never counted to see if anyone is missing!

Had a one and a half-hour transfer to Wuzoulou lodge but it was well worth it. We had a compact room for three, but it was clean and the place had a lovely atmosphere. We showered, changed and met everyone in the courtyard for a BBQ supper. Lots of wine was drunk tonight and a very good meal was had by all. A 40th Birthday party for Brita added to the celebrations. A huge cake organised by Carol, Steve and Mike our CITS representatives and much singing and dancing followed.

Strapped For Cash!

Day 6 Sunday 13th April 2003 – Breast Cancer Care information
Breakfast at Wuzoulou Lodge. Start trek to the Wuzoulou Mountain. Most of today's trek will be walking up the mountain – this is the last part of the Wall area built in Ming dynasty. You will walk the last 5 towers on top of the mountain – altitude 1100m. Trek starts at 300m. Transfer by coach to the Yunhu Hotel (about 30 mins). Total trekking time 5-6 hours. Briefing, dinner and overnight at the Yunhu Hotel.

Breakfast the following morning was served in the courtyard, consisting of fresh orange juice and pancakes. The sun was shining and everyone was anticipating a tough day ahead.

Just as we were leaving that morning, Steve came out into the courtyard with a rolled up T-shirt in his hand. Sandra immediately dived behind Julie and me as she recognised it to be one she had left in our room. The embarrassing thing being that it was not just a T-shirt but also a pair of knickers she had discarded and we anticipated Steve holding them up and asking if anyone recognised them. Lucky for her, he changed his mind and her dignity remained in tact! Every hotel we stayed in had a T-shirt and a pair of Sandra's knickers as a memento. Rather than take them home she had left them behind to make more room in her rucksack for souvenirs. Between the three of us we also managed to leave the maintenance guys a small plumbing problem in the toilet department after each of our nights stays. It must have been something to do with the change in our diet.

We were off the wall all day but endured a mountain climb from 300m to 1100m, mostly shaded by trees and shrubs but again difficult underfoot. This mornings walking was really hard work and seriously steep. The walking poles proved immensely useful for balancing and for digging into the ground above you as you made your way up the side of the mountain. A hot morning but as we were mainly shaded by the trees it made for pleasant walking conditions. Lots of water stops and pauses to admire the views.

We were at the front of the first group and so arrived at the summit a good two hours before the last people. It was gloriously sunny so we recovered by lounging at the top and improving our tans. One of the last women to get to the top had only recently recovered from breast cancer and a gruelling few weeks of chemotherapy. She received serious applause from everybody as she came into view at the top of the mountain.

Di had such determination and finished everyday of the trekking despite thinking at the start of each day that she would not be able to do it. The doctor, Richard had his counselling skills tested persuading her not to give up. She should be very pleased with herself, I am fairly fit and very healthy and found it hard work, she really did herself proud.

The views from the tower at the top of the climb were brilliant and despite a very unladylike descent out of the tower window most of us went to the top of the tower to take in the view. After a long, lazy, lunch break we had another challenge to overcome. We now had to walk across plateaus with sheer drops and this spooked Sandra and several of the other women. We managed to steer them across and then started a serious descent into the valley below. Miles over in the distance we could see a tower high up on the mountains and we could visibly count four towers on the way down.

Knowing we had five towers to complete we were all anxiously watching this high tower getting closer to us as we made our way down. As we came to the bottom of the valley, we had counted four towers and the one high above us was the only other tower in sight we realised that we did indeed have a very steep climb to make!

Just as we were all wondering if we actually had the stamina to climb to the top of this mountain we heard a cry from up ahead that the doctor was needed at the front of the group. The doctor soon ambled down the mountain, passed us and stopped a short distance in front of us. Angelise, one of the fitter, more able trekkers had stumbled and fallen, twisting her knee badly behind her as she landed.

Earlier on in the day Peter had fallen and landed heavily on his shoulder and so the hero of the day before was not able to assist the doctor in carrying Angelise back to base. It was suggested that she tried to hop or walk, but the cry of pain when she attempted this made it an unreasonable request.

The only two ways to get her off the mountain were on a stretcher, which we didn't have, or to carry her. Luckily amongst the group of 74 we had two other real men whom immediately offered to help the doctor carry her the two hours back to base. The rest of us continued on up to the tower and then back down into Wuzoulou valley and on to the lodge. Sandy carried Angelise's rucksack the whole way back to camp as well as her own and refused to let anyone else help her with it. These two girls were our heroes for the day.

As we arrived back at the lodge a make do stretcher was just leaving the area with six Chinese helpers in toe. Today had been extremely hard work and Angelise's accident made us all realise how vulnerable we were when we were miles away from civilisation with only the group as support. The beers waiting for us back at Wuzoulou lodge were the best I have ever tasted and the first two didn't even touch the sides. The three of us were relieved to be in one piece and to have survived another day of our challenge.

Two and a half hours later Angelise was carried back into the courtyard, in incredible pain and devastated that her trekking days were over. We had all been drinking, to keep cool, as it was a very hot day and were in very high spirits. We were eventually transported to our luxury hotel later that evening and Angelise, Fiona and the doctor spent the evening at the local hospital. This was to have been our one night of luxury; the hotel had a swimming pool and a foot masseur to tend our aching feet, but because of the accident it was a fairly subdued meal and everyone retired to bed early.

Tonight I shared a room with Jo, a friend of Di's as they had no three bedders and we were both with two other friends. Jo was lovely and although we didn't get to know each other very well, it was good to talk to somebody else about their reasons for being on the trek. Jo had come in support of Di as she had had a really rough time with breast cancer and they wanted to raise loads of money for such a good cause.

Between the three of them they had got lots of sponsors and wore different T-shirts everyday with the sponsors' names on. Had a really comfortable night and slept through for the first time. Must have had something to do with no snoring from Sandra! I met back up with the girls at breakfast the following day.

Japanese Suits

Day 7 Monday 14th April 2003 – Breast Cancer Care information
After breakfast transfer from Yunhu Lodge to the Black Dragon Pool Park (about 45 mins). Begin today's trek walking up the Black Dragon Pool gorge for approximately 2½ hours. This is mainly easy underfoot but mostly uphill. The walking is partly in the shade and partly exposed. From the plateau at the top of the gorge, continue for 1½ hours, off the beaten track, on local trails with the guide and descend down the other side of the mountain. This section consists of loose rubble, loose soil, and lots of shrubs and under-growth. It would be advisable to wear long trousers if you want to avoid scratched legs. The trek will continue to Jingling Valley and walk up to a waterfall. This we will ascend by climbing up a tread metal stairway that is secured to the side of the rock face. We will then descend and walk to the waterfall resort hotel where we will meet our coach and be transported to the Green Lake hotel for our overnight stay. Transfer approx.1½ hours. Total trekking time 7 hours. Briefing, dinner and overnight at Green Lake.

Our injured colleague was well and truly strapped up at breakfast the following morning and her trekking days were sadly over. The rest of us were promised an easier day although still challenging and we set off for our destination. Our transfer to Black Dragon pool from the Yunhu Hotel took about 45mins.

When we arrived in the gorge it was sunny but refreshingly cool and we followed the river, crossing over huge boulders and bridges for about an hour. We passed a lot of Japanese tourists and there were lots of little stalls selling cool drinks and souvenirs. As we rounded the next corner we came across a cascading waterfall which looked very inviting and many of us were tempted to dangle our weary feet in the cooling waters. A perfect photo spot and so we had a short break before tackling the iron stairs, which took us way up to the top of the waterfall, and to a magnificent view of the gorge below us.

From the plateau at the top we walked for another one and a half hours, off the beaten track – no Japanese tourists in business suits up here. This part of the trek consisted of loose rubble, loose soil, shrubs and scrubby under-growth. We continued on down into the valley and stopped for lunch in the dried up riverbed. Some of us arrived here a good couple of hours before the others so we had lots of time to explore the area or just sit and chill out.

I actually found this morning hard work and my legs really complained about the metal stairs, which seemed to go on forever.

When everyone had arrived, Jo suggested that everybody take ten minutes of quiet time to contemplate why they were on the trek and to remember the people we were actually raising money for. This was a very reflective time for most of us and the three of us said prayers for Celia and the rest of her family and asked that she be given the strength to fight her battle against cancer.

After this break we continued down the valley through a beautifully kept village with lots of healthy looking animals and well tended homes. Orderly houses and animal shelters surrounded us and happy villagers went about their daily chores, waving to the strange white women walking through their village.

Our next surprise was to arrive in Jingling Valley and to find ourselves at the bottom of the highest waterfall in the area. It was quite a spectacular view up the mountain to the top of the waterfall although the rush of water was in fact a bit pathetic and better described as a trickle.

The majority of the group then ascended to the top of the

waterfall by means of a tread metal staircase secured to the side of the mountain. It looked rather precarious snaking up the side attached by metal rivets, but we were assured it was perfectly safe. The view from the top was well worth it despite the disappointing fall of water.

A short walk back down took us to the Waterfall resort hotel where we met our coach and were transported to the Green Lake hotel for our overnight stay. This took about one and a half-hours and many of us slept after a hard days climbing.

The three of us were back together again tonight and we had a massive room with a lounge area as well. Whilst wearing my flip-flops this evening I got my one and only blister of the whole trek. Just goes to show how good my walking boots turned out to be. Supper was similar to the other evenings with a few more fish dishes and we managed to find the bar for a swift beer before we retired to our beds. I shall be sorry to leave this hotel, very comfy night, different breakfast consisting of last night's leftovers and a shower that worked really well.

Shop till You Drop

Day 8 Tuesday 15th April 2003 – Breast Cancer Care information
After breakfast meet in courtyard, carry luggage to coaches in the car park. Transfer by coach (about 10 mins) from Green Lake to the Great Wall at Mutianyu. This is a challenging part of the trek, ending with steps up a steep incline of approx. 70%. The wall has been renovated and here there are some of the best views of the whole challenge. Group photos will be taken here and even a toboggan ride down. All trekkers to meet in the car park, where there may be time to wander around the stalls. From here you will be transferred to Beijing (about 2 hours, depending on traffic). Arrive at the Exhibition Hotel. Total trekking time 4 hours. Dinner in hotel or local restaurant, overnight at Exhibition Hotel.

On our way to our last day of the trek which was to be back on the wall we visited a ceramics factory. We were allowed to see the making of Chinese bowls and vases from the very early stages and it was fascinating to watch the women working so quickly with such intricate pieces of metal. The painting of the ceramics was painstakingly slow in that it took several layers to complete and each layer had to be dry before the next could be added.

After watching the bowls being made we were then let loose in the factory shop where we could buy souvenirs of our visit. I bought a bracelet for myself in a typical Chinese blue colour and two ancient Chinese coins. One of the coins is now placed on our doorstep as I was told it would bring us good luck and fortune – still waiting to win the lottery – the other I gave to Josh and he wears it round his neck on an old piece of leather! Some of the women in the group bought so much stuff they had to buy extra bags to carry things home in.

From the factory we made our way to the Great Wall at

Mutianyu about ten minutes away. This was the first place we had been to where there were dozens of other coaches and cars. It felt very strange to be amongst so many other tourists as we had spent most of the trek so far completely isolated from other people.

To get up to the wall we had to climb approximately 200 steps up a 70% incline! This was challenging to say the least and took some people quite a while. The majority of us made it to the top and the views were breathtaking. In this area most of the wall was intact and the towers were complete which made for stunning images of the wall disappearing in the distance. Lots of photos were taken here and everyone was anticipating the last trek on the wall before our final destination. The sides of the wall were very high, the brickwork very elaborate and both sides of the wall were heavily crenellated (gaps along the top of the wall). Underfoot the bricks were so smooth it was like walking on a camomile lawn

It was all a bit emotional as each individual finished their personal trek on the designated tower and was cheered by the rest of the Breast Cancer Care group. Photos were taken of everyone and some had brought mini bottles of champagne with them to celebrate their individual triumphs. Bit of a slip up there on Sandra's part not to have alcohol on her person! Emotions running high as the last few people finished and made it up the steps to the top of the tower.

Spent a long time at this our final destination, reflecting on what we had done and that we had achieved our aim and completed the challenge. We all excitedly sent text messages home to say that we had just finished the trek. Unfortunately Angelise could not make it up to this point so we had some group photos taken down at the bus later where she had waited patiently for us all morning. The group made their way back down either by toboggan, cable car or walking and then most of us met in a bar at the bottom for a well-earned celebratory beer.

There were lots of market stalls in the area so the group did some serious shopping. I bought a fantastic book on "The Great Wall" and an old wooden plaque with a dragon on. Incredibly cheap and it was difficult to spend money. We had the most amazing battered pancake from a local stall. It had a fried egg in the middle of it and tasted like heaven after all that climbing this morning. Found our way back to the bus for some final group pictures and then taken to the Exhibition Hotel were we would be staying for the next few days.

The hotel was right in the centre of Beijing and the traffic was unbelievable. I have never seen so many bicycles in one place before and the bike parks went on for miles. The city was very noisy and bustling and we were all glad to eventually arrive at the hotel and book into our rooms. Not the nicest we had endured over the week but OK. Tonight we were being taken out to a Chinese restaurant for a slap up meal so we are all putting on our glad rags and trying to find some make up. Picked up by the coaches and taken into the city centre.

The restaurant has a very impressive entrance with massive marble Chinese dogs guarding the doorway. Inside the seating is at huge round tables and the staff are anxiously awaiting our arrival.

Most of the group has made firm friends throughout the trip and people stick together for their meal. As Julie, Sandra and I have been together throughout the whole trip we sat together with Jaquie, Paula and many of the others we have become pals with over the week.

The meal is again delicious and we all tuck in to the three courses offered. The rooms are noisy with chatter and laughter and everyone is sharing their experiences of the last few days. Angelise has managed to hobble her way up to restaurant and is in good spirits. Although in pain she has coped well with the two days she has been immobile and got around as well as she can. Shortly before coming on the trek she was diagnosed with MS so the whole challenge was quite something for her. She is a very positive person and should be proud of the way she has managed. I wish her all the very best in the future.

After the meal we went on a night-time tour of Beijing, visiting Snack Street and the famous Tiananmen Square and Forbidden City from the outside. Snack Street was a sight to be seen with food of every nature being sold and eaten. The stalls were set out along the side of the street for about half a mile and were being well patronised by locals and tourists alike. The stallholders were very keen for us to try their wears but what with the SARS virus being rife in Beijing we were a bit reluctant.

Some of the more exotic delicacies included, octopus, scorpion, stomach lining and seahorse. Sandy, a female pilot who works for Air 2000 and the bravest amongst us, ate a scorpion and insisted it tasted very good. I was not so brave and just had a fruit kebab.

Leaving Snack Street we headed for the famous square in Beijing. It was quite spooky driving round it at night with just the streetlights shining on the building at one end. Remembering what had happened there in 1980 made the whole square a bit intimidating. The Forbidden City was lit from the outside and we could just see the entrance gates to this amazing temple, we would see more tomorrow when we returned for a proper visit.

When we got back to the hotel the majority of the group was getting excited about returning to England the day after tomorrow and Sandra and I began to feel a bit homesick. We asked if it would be possible to change our flight and go back with the main group rather than staying on for the Beijing extension. Carol promised to look into it for us and let us know. The SARS virus had really taken hold and we were anxious to get home while still healthy and the authorities were allowing people to travel from infected areas.

The next bit of news surprised us both when Carol told us that Sandra was already booked to go back on Thursday anyway and it was only my ticket that needed to be changed! After a further twenty four hours wait we were finally told that in fact they had the wrong name for Sandra and we were both due to fly home on Sunday but there was a strong possibility of there being spare seats on the earlier flight.

Bike City

Day 9 Wednesday 16th April – Breast Cancer Care information Breakfast at hotel. Day free to enjoy the city of Beijing or take any excursions that you have pre-booked with your tour leader. Gala Peking duck dinner in restaurant outside hotel.

The following morning we got up a bit later and went down for a lovely breakfast, the atmosphere was a bit more relaxed now, all the hard work was done and everyone was enjoying his or her last days in China. Different style meal with lots of fresh fruit and decent coffee.

The majority of the group opted for a guided tour of Beijing and we set of after breakfast in two coaches into the bike jungle of the city centre. I have never seen so many bicycles in one place, motorised vehicles were well and truly out numbered. Our guide suggested that there were over 3 million bicycles in Beijing with a population of 6 million people. It is the ideal mode of transport in such a flat, sprawling metropolis and a sight to be seen.

Whilst travelling through the outskirts of the city, it was fascinating to see the tradesmen actually carrying out their jobs on the side of the road. I saw several clients sitting on the pavements perched on fold up chairs and draped with a cloth round their necks. The local barbers were performing roadside haircuts for the men on their way to and from work. Shoe shiners were crouched at people's feet polishing smart boots until they could see their faces in them. Food snack stalls and hardware traders peddling their goods from bicycles and live animals running around hoping not to be chosen for supper that night.

As well as the millions of bicycles there was a slightly more sophisticated form of transport, the pedicab, which is a three-wheeled bicycle, which can accommodate one or two passengers in the back plus the driver up front. These ducked and dived between the vehicles and overtook the hoards of cyclists who seemed to swarm like bees around our coach.

Our first stop was Tiananmen Square, which to most of us was the place where the tanks and soldiers, trying to break up the pro-democracy demonstrations killed hundreds of students in 1980. Today the square is a rather dismal place where people wander and some fly kites or buy balloons for the children. The square was a gathering place in the days of Imperial China and the government offices are found here. Today Chairman Mao's body is on display in the Mao Zedong Mausoleum and when we visited the square there was a massive queue of Chinese people waiting to file past the sarcophagus. The Chinese seemed to find Tiananmen Square fascinating but to be honest we found it rather depressing and very drab.

Our next stop was the Forbidden City and this was more appealing to the majority of us. The city was named because it was out of bounds to commoners for over 500 years and contains the largest amount of ancient Chinese buildings in the country.

For some of us the most challenging part of the ten-day trek took place in the Ladies Toilets in the Forbidden City. Being nice English women we all queued up at the entrance to the loos and waited our turn. All of a sudden we heard a lot of Chinese chatter behind us and we were pushed and shoved aside by a group of about a dozen elderly, tiny, Chinese 'ladies'. To start with we all thought maybe some of them were desperate to relieve themselves so kindly stepped aside and let them go first. When it continued to happen we had to resort to pushing our way forward and guarding each other in the loos so that another one of our group could actually get into the loo after us and not be beaten to it by the wily Chinese population. There was much muttering from both sides but we would still be there today if we had let them get away with it.

The buildings in the Forbidden City are beautiful and highly decorated with very bright colours. The city was home to two famous dynasties, the Ming and Qing and most of the Emperors spent the majority of their lives there. The palace has some 800 buildings, living accommodation, libraries, theatres, temples and gardens. It is truly massive and covers an area of some 720,000 sq. metres. The decorative order of the palace amazed me but we later learned that the restoration and maintenance programme goes in a continuous 10 year cycle, so once they reach the end of the list of jobs to do they start back at the beginning again.

Standing alongside one of the temples and looking over the rooftops in the Forbidden City is another unforgettable image I have of my visit to China. Seeing the tiny intricate, mythical and real animals carved on the corners of the rooves, with the magical blue sky behind them was beautiful.

After a visit to the souvenir shop where some of the group shopped for England we took the bus back to the History Museum where we had a delicious lunch. After this we were dropped at the shopping mall for 2 hours and then transferred back to the Hotel for our last evening in Beijing. Again we were taken to a traditional Chinese restaurant and tonight's treat was to be Peking duck.

Several of the group had bought Chinese dresses or jackets for the evenings festivities and it added a real feel to the 'last supper'. Our two Chinese video girls played the tape they had made of our trek and it was very nostalgic to look back over what we had achieved. After our meal there were lots of speeches and mentions of thanks to different people involved and many of the women who had suffered breast cancer spoke about their experiences and of their triumphs in completing the challenge. Everybody who had come on the trek, even those who had not been able to complete the entire 6 days walking were given a certificate by Breast Cancer Care as a reminder of what we had done.

Many tears were shed and it turned into a very emotional few hours. We returned to our hotel all with different thoughts on the ten preceding days and what they meant to us as individuals. Everybody on the trek had a different reason for being there and I believe without exception, we all experienced something we will never regret or forget in a hurry.

Escaping SARS

Day 10 Thursday 17th *April – Breast Cancer Care information Breakfast and meet in hotel lobby with luggage ready to load onto coaches.*
10.15 hours. Transfer to airport
14.05 hours. Depart Beijing on your economy class Air China flight CA 937 to London Heathrow. Total flying time approximately 10 hours. 8 hour time difference.
17.50 hours. Arrive London Heathrow, Terminal 3.

The following morning Sandra and I were told we had got a flight home with the others so we went to pack and collect up our mementoes of the trip. We were pleased to be going back with Julie; it would have been awful seeing her off on the coach and not being with her. We did however have to say lots of goodbyes, many of the women were staying in Beijing and some were going on to the Terracotta Warriors in Xi'an. The journey to the airport was quiet and most people were subdued, lost in memories of the last few days.

I managed to find Ali a Chinese doll dressed in national costume at the airport as she collects them, and found some other bits and pieces to take home for the family.

The flight home was uneventful, we managed to raise some more money for Breast Cancer Care by asking people to donate their Chinese coins to the cause and we also had several people express an interest in walking the Great Wall in 2004.

There were more emotional goodbyes at Heathrow and then through customs to be met by our families. It was fantastic to see husbands and kids waiting to greet us and they all seemed very proud of what we had achieved. Leaving Sandra and Julie to go our separate ways seemed strange, we had done everything together for the last ten days and now we were back to reality. The journey home was noisy, so much to talk about and catch up on. I think they really missed me and I had a fabulous greeting from my faithful training partner, Mollie when we got home. Seems strange being home, my bed is so comfy and it's great to be back with the family, but I miss the girls.

The fact that the three of us travelled together and because of the situation with Celia at home, meant that we kept to ourselves and didn't integrate with some of the other trekkers. To be honest there were some people on the trip that I never even spoke to. To some extent I regret that, although I guess it was inevitable that we would not get to know everyone. The people we did meet and chat to all had their own reasons for being there and some were happy to share those experiences. Julie, Sandra and I felt very protective towards Celia and although some of the girls we made friends with knew the situation, not many of the group knew the reasons for our challenge. On our return are fears were confirmed and we were all saddened by the deterioration in Celia's condition.

2 months after our return

Celia is not at all well and we are all very concerned for her. She has to undergo operations to clear her lungs and she is very weak. Sandra has been up to see her and was very upset at seeing her that way. Julie has been in touch and still seems hopeful that they will be able to sort her out but I am beginning to have serious doubts. She is very weak and the fight seems to have gone out of her.

 3 months after our return

Yet another set back with Celia this week, she is in a lot of pain so they are admitting her to a hospice to try and get her pain under control with more morphine. The last day of the school term and Josh's last at primary school. Sandra is very low and feeling helpless, I think she is now coming to terms with what is inevitable and is finding it hard to accept. Spoke to her several times over the weekend and she is trying to keep positive.

29th July 2003

Phoned Sandra today after work to hear the news that Celia had died in the night, only a couple of weeks after her 40th birthday. She went into a deep sleep on Sunday and never really became fully conscious again. I feel so saddened that she fought such a hard battle and still did not survive this cruel disease and that poor Julie has to go through losing another close family member. Her Mum died of breast cancer several years before and now she has to go through it all again. I spent some of the day with Sandra; we were both very tearful about Celia's death and the waste of such a young life, but relief that she was out of pain at last.

Challenge complete

So very glad that we completed the Great Wall of China Trek. Feel proud that we rose to the challenge and met some great, courageous people in the process. Only wish there had been a happier ending for Julie and her family and that we could have made more of a difference for them.

The Breast Cancer Care group, who completed the China Trek 2003 walked for 36 hours, climbed 9,000 steps and covered a distance of 90km. Between us we raised nearly £250,000. There were 70 women, 4 men, 3 CITS reps, 2 Breast Cancer Care reps, 2 tour reps and a doctor. Ages ranged from 18 years to over 60.

Everyone had different challenges and fears to overcome during the 10 days away. Jacqui was spending her first nights away from her husband in 30 years. Many of us were leaving young children behind for the first time and some of the group had fears of flying. This was all before we even reached China and we had 6 days of trekking infront of us. Some people found being part of such a large group a struggle and others had travelled alone so knew nobody when they arrived at the airport.

The challenges of the trek aroused new fears in the group. Many people found new friends amongst them and no doubt formed life long friendships, while others didn't mix well and may have had a lonely experience during the trip. While the climbing of 9000 steps was my biggest worry, the vastness and insecurity of a lot of the remote areas was a problem for others. Several of the women had definite anxieties about the height and vulnerability of some of the stretches and needed coaxing and reassurance from others to alleviate their fears. By the end of the 10 days I would imagine most of these apprehensions would have been overcome and added to the satisfaction of completing the Great Wall Trek. I'm sure the majority would remember it as a very worthwhile experience.

If you have enjoyed reading my journal or have any comments to make please contact me on janewaugh2000@yahoo.co.uk.
Further copies can be obtained from www.lulu.com and www.amazon.co.uk

www.ingramcontent.com/pod-product-compliance
Lightning Source LLC
Chambersburg PA
CBHW021211020426
42331CB00003B/313